ESTERN RAILWAY.

T CARRIAGES

Y'S TRAIN

to WINDSOR,

Y, THE 7TH NOVEMBER, 1900.

18/20

INCES OPOLD AND AURICE OF FENBERG AND NDANTS. HEOBALD.	SIR ARTHUR BIGGE. SIR THOMAS DENNEHY. CAPT. PONSONBY. SURGEON BANKART.	MAJOR COLBORNE. HERR VON PFYFFER. INDIAN ATTENDANTS.	FOR PAGES AND UPPER SERVANTS.	DIRECTORS.	DIRECTORS.	FOURGON.	GUARD.
LOON. 50.	SALOON. No. 131.	SALOON. No. 71.	SALOON. No. 72.	SALOON. No. 180.	CARRIAGE No. 306.	TRUCK. No. 100.	VAN. No. 272.

403 feet 5 inches →

Palaces on Wheels

*HM King Edward VII descending at Newcastle from the then
fairly new London & North Western Railway Royal train, 1906.*

Palaces on Wheels

Royal Carriages at the National Railway Museum

David Jenkinson and Gwen Townend

London: Her Majesty's Stationery Office

HM Queen Elizabeth II boarding the Royal Train at Aberdeen, 1978. The vehicle featured is the new principal saloon of 1977, the construction of which, along with additional supporting vehicles, was the prime cause of the release to the National Railway Museum of fully half the preserved collection of Royal Train vehicles which form the subject of this book.

*HM Queen Victoria's London & North Western Railway Royal
Train and crew in the pre-1895 era. It is seen waiting for duty
on the former Midland Railway behind one of the graceful,
Johnson-built engines of this system.*

Contents

The London & North Western Railway's Royal Train at Ollerton on the Lancashire, Derbyshire & East Coast Railway in 1906. HM King Edward VII was attending the St Leger race meeting at Doncaster on this occasion.

Authors' Preface

The writers of this book are unashamed monarchists, so we have counted it a great privilege and pleasure to have been closely associated, since 1975, with the development and restoration of the preserved collection of Royal Train vehicles now in the custody of the National Railway Museum at York. Moreover, working as we do in the educational and library departments of the Museum we have been particularly concerned with the research into the history of the vehicles and their subsequent presentation and interpretation to millions of visitors. By now, the coaches to us are old friends.

Over the past few years, the numerous enquiries the Museum has received about the royal saloons suggests that our own affection for the vehicles is shared by many. This feeling, coupled with the considerable enlargement of the collection during 1978 and 1979 has prompted the hope that a special publication, attempting to explain something of the history of the preserved collection, might be of interest and value. Furthermore, the mere fact of writing it would serve as a useful spur to our conducting further research into many additional parts of the story. Thus, encouraged by the Director of our parent body, the Science Museum, and the Keeper of the National Railway Museum itself, we have attempted to put together a reasonably detailed survey of what are, after all, some of the most priceless relics in the Museum's care.

We are, of course, in the very fortunate position of enjoying unrestricted access to the whole of the collection but, from the outset, we must make it clear that at the time of writing it is not normally possible for the Museum to place all the vehicles on show simultaneously without seriously upsetting the total historical 'balance' of the main display hall. As a general rule, therefore, visitors will only find a selection of the vehicles on public show. Consequently it is our prime hope that this book, by attempting to put *all* the vehicles in their historical perspective, will enable our visitors to understand more fully those particular examples which are on show at any one time.

DJ/AGT
National Railway Museum
1981

Introduction

In 1849, Queen Adelaide Amelia Louisa Theresa Caroline, sister of the Duke of Saxe-Meiningen, and widow of the late King William IV, was laid to rest. More than fifty years of Queen Victoria's reign were still to come and the fully mechanised railway was scarcely twenty years old when the Dowager Queen died; yet throughout the length and breadth of Britain, railway lines had been spreading their tentacles at a rate which, even in the late twentieth century, beggars the imagination. Many of the principal private railway companies which were to become veritable giants before the nineteenth century was over were already in existence. At the Wolverton Works of one of them, the fledgling London & North Western Railway, some unnamed and unknown railway officer seems to have resolved that Queen Adelaide's railway carriage, now no longer needed, was too good to be broken up and saw to it that it was tucked into some quiet corner, out of harm's way. Thus began a process of preserving and conserving the principal railway saloons of all subsequent British monarchs (and their families) which has continued uninterrupted until the present day and which has resulted in the British National Railway Museum at York becoming the custodian of the largest, finest and most varied collection of royal railway vehicles anywhere in the world.

Like most collections, its existence at all is a combination of accident and design. No one now knows why Queen Adelaide's saloon was spared from the breakers. At the time there was no real national feeling that the new railway industry was going to be so economically and socially significant as to merit the systematic preservation of some of its more noteworthy artifacts for posterity – such realisation was not to occur until more modern days. Yet, unprompted by either government decree or enthusiast pressure groups nor, apparently, influenced by even an official decision on the part of senior railway management, many generations of craftsmen at Wolverton saw to it that Saloon No 2 was handed down to the succeeding custodians in good order. Although it was exhibited from time to time, it was not until more than a century after the Dowager Queen's death (in 1963 to be precise) and against very changed public attitudes to historic vehicles that the carriage was placed on permanent public exhibition in a museum – the former Museum of British Transport – at Clapham in South London. There it was joined by other and later royal vehicles to form the nucleus of the present collection and transferred with them to York for the opening of the National Railway Museum by HRH The Duke of Edinburgh in September 1975. Early in

These views show many of the, now preserved, vehicles in use in their heyday. Above, the London, Midland & Scottish Railway (formerly London & North Western Railway) train is seen at Ballater on the London & North Eastern Railway in the 1920s. The first three vehicles are all now preserved. Below, the East

Coast train is seen in British Railways days in May 1953 behind the appropriately named Eastern Region Royal Train locomotive Royal Sovereign. *Of the first four vehicles, only the second (a semi-royal saloon) does not survive in the National Collection. The coaches are still in the pre-BR varnished teak livery.*

1979, the story (to date) was nicely completed when the Museum received the most modern addition to its royal collection so far – the very same saloon in which Prince Philip had travelled to open the Museum and which had, originally, been built in 1941 for his father-in-law, HM King George VI.

Although the Museum has this fine collection in its care, it should perhaps be made clear from the outset that many royal and semi-royal vehicles have not survived for posterity to see – although the Museum does possess odd items of furniture and fittings from some of them. Nevertheless, between Queen Adelaide's saloon and the 'modern' saloons of 1941 stand some ten other preserved vehicles of royal status or with royal association, spanning a century of progress, development and social change. This is the story of these preserved vehicles.

Restoration work in progress on the Royal Train vehicles, showing repainting of a support vehicle, replacement of Royal Crest on HM King Edward VII's saloon and panel replacement on HM Queen Alexandra's saloon.

1 The Victorian Age

Queen Adelaide

From almost the earliest days of the fully mechanised railway, members of the British Royal Family have been inveterate train travellers – none more so than HM Queen Victoria, who took her first ride on a train as early as 1842, in company with Prince Albert. She is said to have been 'quite charmed'; but it was her aunt, the Dowager Queen Adelaide, for whom the first genuine royal saloon was provided – London & Birmingham Railway carriage No 2. *En passant* it is worth mentioning that no one seems to know why it was given this number – no recorded mention of a carriage No 1 has, thus far, been located by the Museum.

There is some slight confusion about the age of Queen Adelaide's saloon. It is generally assigned an 1842 building date but it is known that the Dowager Queen made her first rail journey in 1840 and it seems a little improbable that the railway would commission two different carriages in the space of two years – vehicle technology was not advancing at quite such a rapid pace. Furthermore, the coach is so much a typical early vehicle that it is at least probable that it was not

built as such for the Queen but converted from a standard first-class carriage. It is quite possible that the 1842 date refers to such conversion, the earlier 1840 journey having taken place in an unconverted vehicle – possibly even the same carriage.

Be that as it may, it is known that the vehicle body was built by the firm of Hoopers of Gough Street, London – the same Hoopers traditionally associated with road travel and whose motorcar bodies have in more modern times frequently been associated with royal motor vehicles. Unfortunately, the original building records cannot be traced. The most significant point about Queen Adelaide's coach is the fact that it was just about the most up-to-date vehicle possible to build at the time of its construction. Apart from the fact that it was built by an outside firm (the only preserved royal saloon to have this distinction), it set a precedent for virtually all succeeding royal vehicles. Although the passage of time imparts a period quality to all vehicles, it was always the railway tradition to offer the monarch the most up-to-date technology whenever new carriages were brought into service. In consequence, the preserved collection accurately encapsulates all that was best in railway vehicle technology throughout the period.

Queen Adelaide's coach, therefore, truly represents the 'stage coach' influence on railway carriage building and is undoubtedly the finest surviving example of the genre even without its royal associations. Early carriages derived both their shape and nomenclature from the stage coach era – and were not infrequently built in the same workshops as their road ancestors. Essentially the general principle was to mount what were effectively three road coach bodies (generally called compartments) on one four wheel railway chassis. Interior detail varied according to the class of traveller and the preserved coach displays the most wonderfully elaborate brocade upholstery, thick carpeting and heavily tasselled hangings. Its seating capacity is very limited (ten only) and the body itself is noticeably narrower than the chassis – reflecting the fact that at this early stage of development, the

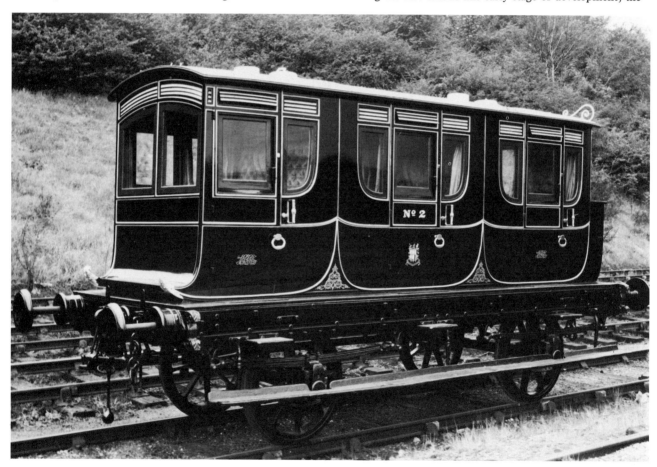

railways had hardly begun to exploit the dimensional possibilities offered by a rail vehicle whose stability was far better than the road equivalent. Strictly speaking, the vehicle has only two proper compartments, the third element being a half (or coupé) section with end facing windows. This was to permit a box-like extension (or boot) at the other end which on some vehicles was used to house mails, but in this example allowed the compartment to be converted to night use by raising a connecting flap to the boot and inserting a separate cushion between a pair of facing seats, thus permitting the occupants to lie down with their feet projecting beyond the normal extremities of the compartment. All these details were common features of the best first-class carriages of the day, Queen Adelaide's carriage being different solely in the quality of upholstery and furnishing. It is, therefore, properly referred to as a bed carriage.

The guard would ride on the roof (again characteristic of the period) whereon would also be carried any luggage; while the

Exterior of HM Queen Adelaide's saloon, clearly showing the 'stage coach' origins of vehicle styling in the early mechanised railway age.

The ingenious sleeping arrangement in Queen Adelaide's coach.

vehicle itself is carried on fully sprung, cast iron spoked wheels suspended by road carriage type leaf springs. End shocks were absorbed by telescopic sprung buffers at each corner padded at their extremities in leather but the vehicle has no brakes. The exterior decoration, all applied by hand, is lavish, but not untypical of railway practice generally. The decorative insignia are those of the London & Birmingham Railway which owned the vehicle. The exterior colour scheme is dark red and black, the dark red being associated with royal railway travel and which finds its modern equivalent not only on the Royal Train but on royal road vehicles and some of the aircraft of the Queen's Flight. Certain exterior fittings are gold plated reflecting its royal status.

The Museum possesses no records of the method of employment of the vehicle. However, being unbraked, it clearly must have operated as part of a train containing other, lesser vehicles and indeed this would have been necessary to carry all the members of the Queen's household. It seems likely that the Queen herself (probably with her closest companion) rode in the coupé end by day and the bed compartment at night, leaving the central compartment for her other close attendants.

The carriage was withdrawn from service after the Queen's death in 1849 and thereafter carefully conserved at the Wolverton Works of the London & North Western Railway (LNWR), formed in 1846 as a result of the amalgamation of several smaller systems, including the London & Birmingham line. From time to time it was brought out for special exhibitions and a particularly noteworthy example was its journey to the 1904 Exposition in St Louis, USA, where it was accompanied by a fine model (which has also survived and is in the Museum) of the then new King Edward VII saloon. Such was the care bestowed on the old carriage down

Attention to detail was and is always a feature of royal saloons. These three typical examples from Queen Adelaide's vehicle show that this trend was established at an early date.

the years that when it finally went on permanent public show in 1963 it was virtually as good as when withdrawn some 114 years earlier – a truly remarkable tribute to the dedication of hundreds of railwaymen down the years.

Queen Victoria

If Queen Adelaide's carriage is most noteworthy for its commonality with normal coaching stock of the period, the same cannot really be said of the next vehicle in the story – HM Queen Victoria's saloon. By the time it was constructed in 1869, Queen Victoria had been a regular rail user for over 26 years and had distinctly clear notions as to what she expected of a royal railway conveyance. As early as 1858 she had complained to the LNWR of excessive heat in the royal saloon she was then using and by 1868 she had offered to pay the LNWR the sum of £800 in order to carry out substantial alterations to her vehicles. The company resolved to 'adapt the two existing vehicles as family carriages and build new ones for the Queen at a cost of £1000 in addition to this subsidy of £800.' The Queen agreed. As a result it would be neither disloyal nor inaccurate to state that the quite remarkable vehicle resulting from this joint enterprise is one of the most noteworthy pieces of social history in the collection. As far as is known it is the only British royal vehicle whose constructional costs have been met in part by the reigning monarch of the day. But not only did it closely follow the Queen's personal wishes, it also embodied in its construction several innovative features in the field of railway vehicle technology. It was designed by Richard Bore of the LNWR and built at Wolverton as two separate vehicles, each mounted on six wheels. This was the logical progression (in Britain at least) from the earlier 4-wheel style and of itself was not innovative. What was new was the sound insulation below the floorboards and the fact that a flexible gangway connected the two vehicles together, the first time this had occurred in Britain. It is said that, convenient though this was, the Queen mistrusted the arrangement and insisted that the train be brought to a standstill before she would move through the gangway from her day saloon to the bedroom area. In 1895 the ensemble was modernised and rebuilt by joining the two bodies together on a single 12-wheel chassis and as such it survives.

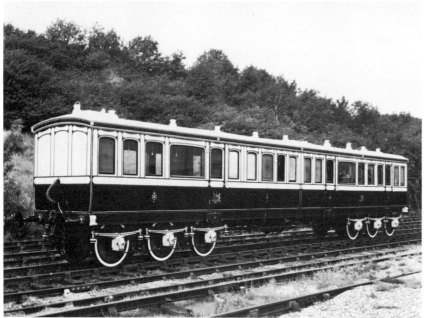

HM Queen Victoria's saloon seen in pre- and post-1895 condition. The skilful uniting of the two elements on one chassis is marked on the rebuilt version by a crown on the cornice moulding and the double line of vertical panel beading at the centre line.

HM Queen Victoria's bedroom in the preserved saloon. It is presumed that the slightly smaller bed was used by whichever royal princess was accompanying the Queen.

Queen Victoria had the use of several royal saloons – for it was the practice of the larger private railways each to provide its own Royal Train vehicles – but only the LNWR vehicle now exists. This is probably because it was her undoubted favourite and she herself had a great deal of influence (as have had all subsequent monarchs) in the original design. In this respect it is one of the more curious facets of British royal rail travel that, although the railways actually owned the vehicles, the coaches themselves were exclusively for the Royal Family and designed to meet their wishes.

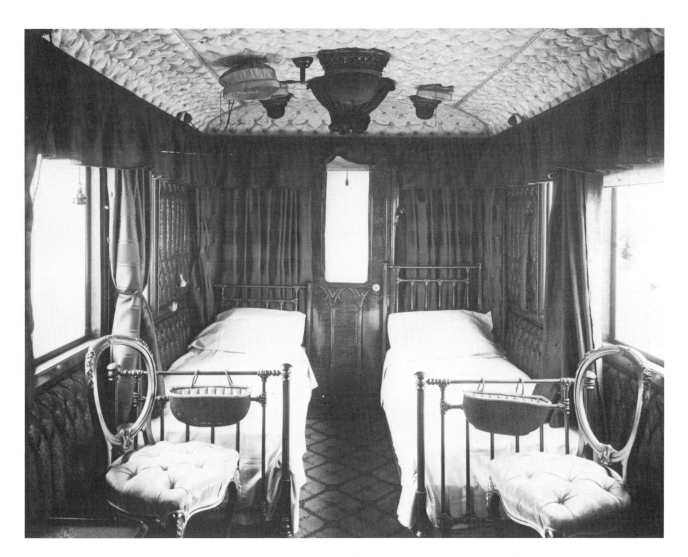

Queen Victoria's saloon (and hereafter it will be referred to in the singular) was designed to meet the Queen's specific travelling needs. It is the oldest of the preserved vehicles to truly merit the 'Palace on Wheels' description for indeed that is what it is. It consists essentially of a day and night saloon for the Queen (separated by a toilet area) and extra accommodation for her immediate retinue. At one end a small four-seat compartment (with adjoining toilet) was provided for her principal retainer. This was used originally by the Queen's celebrated manservant, John Brown, whose

The hand-painted Order of St Patrick and carved lion's head on Queen Victoria's saloon.

legendary instructions, prefaced always by 'The Queen says . . .', have become part of folklore.

John Brown used the compartment only in the days when the coach was two 6-wheelers, for he died in 1883. His place in later years was taken by the equally celebrated Indian Abdul Karim (the Munshi). Perhaps it was at this time in history that the tea-brewing equipment was installed – we do not know. The Queen would never eat on the train – it had to stop at selected stations for meal breaks – but, apparently, she would make an exception in the case of a cup of tea.

Leading out of the attendant's compartment is the main day saloon – a veritable cornucopia of Victoriana at its most opulent. The woodwork is bird's-eye maple, the upholstery is blue watered silk and the ceilings have white quilted silk linings. As far as records indicate, these were the Queen's personal choice and the upholstery silk is truly 'royal' blue. It is not the most relaxing place one can envisage – it was more of a royal workroom. True, there are settees and armchairs but there are also writing desks – it would seem that the Queen's propensity for writing her journals was not to be interrupted by such mundane considerations as rail travel. Victorian this saloon may be, but restful it is not – at least to the modern eye.

Beyond the day saloon is a small toilet/washing compartment and then the royal bed chamber – this time decorated in red damask. Prince Albert – a great pioneer in rail travel – had died before this vehicle was built but there are nevertheless two beds in the coach; for the Queen always travelled with one of her close family. It seems that it was a highly privileged distinction to share the sleeping saloon with the Queen and in the preserved vehicle the honour seems to have been divided between Princess Louise from 1869 until her marriage, then Princess Beatrice (even after her marriage) and finally Princess Victoria, daughter of the Prince of Wales, later HM King Edward VII.

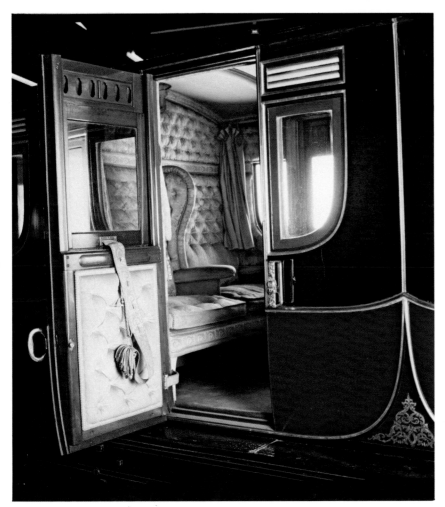

*Embroidery and silk brocade in profusion
– Queen Adelaide's carriage.*

*The bed compartment end of Queen
Adelaide's carriage.*

*The coupé (or chariot) end of Queen
Adelaide's carriage.*

Following page:

*Victoria Regina, and no doubt about it –
the principal day compartment of the
Queen's saloon, furnished entirely to the
Queen's choosing and exactly as she last
used it in 1900.*

On 6 June 1889, the train departed for Balmoral – a somewhat ritualistic progress – and Princess Victoria reported to her mother (later Queen Alexandra):

'Balmoral, June 7 . . . After Leamington, where we had some tea, I "turned in" & a lovely soft bed it was too – one quite forgot that one was really in the train. I never saw anything so perfect in arrangement & comfort. Of course you know the carriage well – I do wish you had one like it. I was just dozing off, when Grandmama came to bed – & how it reminded me of you, my Mother. She looked so clean & dear – all in white – & it took some time before she was settled – the shawls, & cushions – then the lamps to put out then again, it felt too hot – then not warm enough, & in the night – Annie was called many a time – to bring her something to drink etc. Oh! it did remind me so of our travels. Well finally we had some sleep, & in the morning I dressed first, so as to make room – & then we soon reached Perth, where the same breakfast awaited us, as you & I enjoyed, some years ago.'

Princess Victoria's wish that her mother should have a carriage like it was to come true in no uncertain fashion some fourteen years later as will be seen in the next chapter.

The last section of Queen Victoria's carriage is taken up by a sort of withdrawing room for her ladies-in-waiting – still displaying bird's-eye maple woodwork but upholstered, like the attendant's compartment, in gold silk, heavily buttoned down. It contains inward-facing settees of a somewhat straight-backed nature and an adjoining washroom. Dominant in one corner is a large electric bell connected to the Queen's apartments and dating from the aforementioned modernisation of the vehicle in 1895.

This latter event was highly typical of Queen Victoria's approach to rail travel. The railway was very anxious to build her a completely new vehicle but she liked her old coaches and would have none of it. However, she did agree to the uniting of the two bodies on one modern chassis, which was done. The railway, thinking to be helpful, also installed modern electric lights and bells but the Queen was less pleased than had been expected. Characteristically she approved of the new bells to summon her attendants but insisted on the re-instatement of the old oil and candle lamps alongside the more modern appliances!

In this form, the coach served out the last six years of the Queen's reign. She made her last journey in it from Balmoral in November 1900 and early in 1901 she died. The old carriage was finally pensioned off alongside Queen Adelaide's saloon – a new era in royal rail travel was about to begin.

Queen Victoria's Ladies-in-Waiting also travelled in some style, although the electric bell (top right) indicates the real state of affairs. Their toilet compartment is beyond the door at the far end.

2 The Edwardian Vehicles

By far the largest group in the preserved collection of royal vehicles originated during the reign of HM King Edward VII, the Museum possessing no fewer than eight vehicles built between 1900 and 1909, quite a number of which were used well into the reign of HM Queen Elizabeth II.

The story of these vehicles properly begins in the late Victorian period. King Edward VII was sixty years old when he succeeded to the throne and, as Prince of Wales, was a frequent and regular user of the railway. He had his own carriages both in Britain and on the continent and, although none survive from this period, it is clear from archive photographs that his vehicles displayed somewhat different ideas regarding rail travel than those of his mother. Consequently when he became King in his own right he knew exactly what he wanted.

The railways had hoped to build new vehicles for Queen Victoria but she had declined the offer. King Edward VII had no such inhibitions and the railways were only too willing to display their finest coachbuilding talents for the benefit of the new monarch. Fortunately for posterity, their best efforts have survived.

The Duke of Sutherland's Saloon

The design of the Edwardian vehicles was undoubtedly influenced by that of a slightly earlier and quite superb vehicle designed by C. A. Park and built in 1899 at Wolverton for His Grace the 4th Duke of Sutherland – a wealthy Scottish landowner who had the right to operate his own private saloon on the railway system. It was kept at Dunrobin Castle and although not a royal saloon *per se*, the vehicle was used by the Duke to entertain more crowned heads of Europe than seem to have enjoyed any other British vehicle – and King Edward VII undoubtedly rode in it at some time. It too survives in the Museum collection as the result of a remarkably astute purchase by the former British Railways Curator of Historical Relics, who obtained it in 1957 for the sum of £350. It originally cost £5000 to build! Since its influence on subsequent royal vehicles was so profound, it seems wholly appropriate to include it in this survey.

The Duke's saloon was built to the most modern specification possible in 1899. It was fitted with two separate swivelling sets of wheels, or bogies (by then the 'norm' for carriage construction, following the earlier 4- and 6-wheel stages) and inside the coach, the decoration is somewhat reminiscent of the Adam style – making much use of white enamel and brighter furnishing fabrics than in the mid-Victorian period. The coach has electric lights as standard and its own self-contained solid fuel central heating system since it frequently operated as a single unit in Scotland. It

could, however, be attached easily to a normal service train for more long-distance travelling such as overnight journeys from north of Inverness to London.

It seems likely that it was the overnight capability and self-contained nature of the vehicle which probably appealed most to King Edward VII – for the coach contains not only lavish day and night accommodation but also a small kitchen-cum-pantry wherein quite elaborate meals could be prepared and still can for that matter, for everything still works. It will be appreciated that Edward VII did not share his mother's alleged dislike of meals on the train.

A final point which may well have appealed to the King was the undoubted elegance of the exterior styling. Built of wood, on a steel chassis, the coach body displays a sort of modified gothic appearance with an abundance of well-proportioned

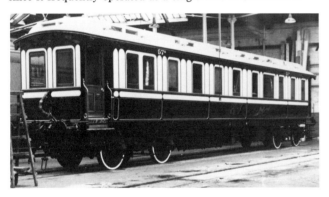

The exterior and principal day compartment of His Grace the Duke of Sutherland's saloon – the trend-setter for the Edwardian vehicles.

panelling – vertical above the waist and horizontal below, all enhanced by a superb two-colour livery of dark 'invisible' green and white, extensively picked out with gilt lining. Window frames are of polished wood; while entrance is gained solely at the extremities of the vehicle by means of set-back, almost ceremonial doors in highly polished mahogany. The whole vehicle is topped by a distinctive clerestory roof (that is, with a raised centre section), domed downwards at the ends. This was a familiar feature on many railway carriages of the time and served both to increase the light and spaciousness of the interior and to enhance the ventilation of the vehicle.

The First Edwardian Royal Saloons

Not surprisingly, when the LNWR (which had built the Duke's saloon) enquired of King Edward VII whether he would like a replacement for the Victorian royal saloon, the King was distinctly enthusiastic and clearly wished to follow the pattern of the Duke of Sutherland's saloon. There is also a persistent story that the King asked for the new vehicles to be made 'as nearly like the Royal Yacht as possible'. The story cannot be verified from the surviving official records but it seems characteristic enough.

The result was the emergence in 1902 of what many regard as the finest examples of railway carriage building ever achieved in Britain – the LNWR royal saloons of King Edward VII, one each for the King and his Queen, again designed by Mr Park. They formed the centrepiece of a magnificent new train, being regularly accompanied on their journeys by up to six more semi-royal saloons of almost equal magnificence for use by the Royal Household and railway officers. One of these, too, survives but in private ownership.

The royal saloons themselves were, in effect, an enlargement of the Duke of Sutherland's vehicle. They were larger and heavier and carried on six-wheel bogies, but stylistically they copied the ducal vehicle. The two colour livery was, of course, that of the owning company (the LNWR) and identical to the colour scheme of Queen Victoria's saloon – a dark carmine lake (dark maroon) on the lower panels and bluish-white above the waist. The whole exterior was elaborately gilded. Carved lions' heads appeared on door handles and chassis ends and each vehicle carried no fewer than eight hand-painted heraldic embellishments – four royal

Paddington 1937 – and HM King George VI is now on the throne – but his grandfather's train has hardly changed.

18

*HM King Edward VII's day
compartment as built – LNWR 1902.*

*King Edward VII's bedroom as built,
1902.*

coats of arms and one each of the four principal orders of British chivalry (Garter, Thistle, Bath and St Patrick).

Inside the vehicles the finishes were equally opulent. Superb individual items of furniture were set off by gold fittings in the day saloons and silver in the bedrooms. Each vehicle had a suite of bedroom, dressing-room and day saloon, together with an end compartment for the footman. The vehicles normally ran as a pair, day saloons adjoining, and entrance was gained by double-width solid mahogany ceremonial doors leading to a carpeted lobby panelled in mahogany. In most respects the coaches were a 'pigeon pair' but the King's day saloon and bedroom were slightly smaller than those in the Queen's coach in order to allow space for a smoking compartment at one end. This lovely little room – one might almost call it a 'snug' – is the only area (apart from the entrance lobbies) where natural wood veneers form the major feature of the décor. It needs very little imagination to

picture its use after dinner when the King returned to his green leather armchair, brandy and cigars at the ready.

These saloons set a totally new style for royal travel and a more detailed description is not out of place, for they established the sort of facilities which have been copied, with very little change, throughout succeeding generations of royal vehicles save, of course, for changing fashions in interior décor.

King Edward VII's alleged wish to have the vehicles like the Royal Yacht (at least in terms of interior styling) seems to have been met, for the bulk of the interior wall finishes were rendered in white enamel in a combination of gloss and eggshell finish. In contemporary sources it was referred to as the 'colonial' style although some other references also compare the effect to that which was created in an earlier age by Robert Adam. The loose furniture was provided by Waring of London, who were the ancestors of Waring & Gillow. They also furnished the Royal Yacht. The furniture itself is in a beautiful satinwood inlaid with ivory. The pieces are generally lighter than in the Victorian era and the whole impression given is one of space, bearing in mind the very restricted dimensions (in absolute terms) of any railway carriage. All upholstery was in varied shades of green as was the carpet; while the bedstead, embellished with the King's monogram was in plated silver.

Ancillary fitments took full account of advancing technology. Thus there were 3-speed pivoting electric fans and electric radiators, in addition to the normal steam heat radiators found in most contemporary railway vehicles. The aforementioned smoking saloon was particularly well finished. Here the predominant white enamel gives way to magnificently matched fiddle-back mahogany panelling inlaid and cross-banded with rosewood and satinwood. Gilt fittings are unburnished, to aid the restful effect, and the armchairs are upholstered in green leather. Originally, there were even electric cigar lighters, the socket outlets for which are still

present. It is said that the King 'much delighted' spectators in the way he made use of this saloon – one footman to light his cigar and a second to adjust the windows and curtains exactly to his liking. It would seem that this little room was also the favourite day-time spot for King George V and Queen Mary, who spent most of their journeys in its elegant surrounds.

The Queen's saloon was substantially similar in terms of general fittings but was designed for both Queen Alexandra herself and Princess Victoria, obviously still a keen rail traveller (see page 15). There were thus two beds in the main sleeping apartment and these were both heavily draped with pink silk hangings suspended from the ceilings. This made the room rather oppressive and Queen Mary had the drapes removed very soon after she took over the vehicle. The sequence of rooms in the Queen's saloon was slightly different in that there was a small dressing-room on either side of the main bedroom – one for the Queen and one for the Princess.

White enamel was again the principal wall finishing treatment, apart from the entrance lobbies, the only areas with natural wood panelling. Just as the predominant fabric colour in the King's saloon was green, the predominant shade in the Queen's coach was blue with pink trimmings and light shades. Carpets were peacock blue at this time.

The outer lobbies of both vehicles – i.e. those at the ends away from the day saloons – were for the footmen's use and contained a pull-out bed/chair plus electrical switchgear and the essential kettle.

The bedroom fittings in the vehicles were designed to be removed when required to enable these rooms to be converted for day use. As far as we can determine, this option was regularly exercised in these two vehicles during the first twenty years of their life but less often thereafter. This may have been because of the changing role of the matching East Coast saloons – see below (page 33).

The footman's compartment, King Edward VII's saloon, 1902. In later years (and as preserved) the positions of chair and cabinet were transposed and the seat upholstered in green leather.

HM Queen Alexandra's bedroom in the LNWR saloon of 1902, showing the elaborate bed drapes for herself and Princess Victoria – all subsequently removed at HM Queen Mary's instruction.

The saloons were built in a space of six months and one contemporary source in 1902 describes them as an elegant Christmas present for His Majesty. They were delivered slightly ahead of the festive season, being used for the first time during the second week of December 1902 on the occasion of a visit by the King and Queen to the Earl and Countess Howe at Gopsall Hall, Leicester.

These two vehicles formed the central element of the Royal Train for almost forty years and their subsequent history under later monarchs is quite complex and can only be summarised here. During the reign of King George V and Queen Mary, the train was regularly used as a mobile home for several days (especially during World War I) and one dressing-room in each saloon was converted into a bathroom with silver-plated bath. These were the first bathrooms fitted to any British railway coaches and were installed in 1915. The second dressing-room in the Queen's saloon became a small sleeping area for the Queen's dresser. Queen Mary also supervised the re-upholstery and re-curtaining of the vehicles during the 1920s – although as already stated, the ornate bed drapes provided for Queen Alexandra had already been removed. It is in this state that the saloons are presented and the present fawn and green carpets are also believed to date from Queen Mary's redecoration. At some time, telephones were added which could be connected to a land line when the train was at rest and a radio appeared in the King's saloon during 1935. This is located in a piece of matching satinwood furniture, which may well have been in the vehicle (probably as a cupboard) from an earlier date.

King Edward VIII did not use the train during his brief reign but when King George VI ascended the throne further modernisation soon took place. In 1938, both carriages were given heavier duty wheels and axleboxes, together with replacement buffing and drawgear – these mechanical improvements probably resulting from the higher speeds at which the train was now operated, given the more modern motive power of the later 1930s. Modernisation was also

The King's and Queen's dressing-rooms in the 1902 saloons. The King's saloon shows the original arrangement and the Queen's shows the new bath installed in 1915 for

applied to some of the supporting vehicles of the Royal Train, also preserved, which will be considered later.

A striking and obvious feature of the LNWR royal saloons and the whole of the associated Royal Train for that matter, was the fact that until 1939 they still carried the colours of the London & North Western Railway. In 1923, the many privately owned railways in Britain had been amalgamated to form four big private companies and the LNWR became the largest constituent of the newly formed London, Midland & Scottish Railway (LMS). The chosen carriage livery of the new system was a rich crimson lake, lined in gilt and vermilion and King George V was duly informed that the Royal Train was about to be repainted in this new scheme. The exact form of this notification is not known, nor the precise reply but his alleged reaction was, essentially, 'Why? I like it as it is.' As a result the old colours were retained (save for the new company markings) during the 1920s and 1930s. The LMS allocated fleet numbers to the saloons in 1933, the King's saloon becoming No 800 and the Queen's

801. Interestingly, although never likely to operate again, Queen Victoria's saloon was officially allocated No 802.

The onset of World War II and the risk of air attack gave great concern to the railways – especially with the Royal Train being now the only set of vehicles carrying the striking carmine lake and white colour scheme and consequently very conspicuous. Accordingly, HM King George VI agreed to the vehicles being painted in the standard crimson lake colour (thus rendering them similar in looks to thousands of other coaches). Thus painted, saloons 800/1 continued in sole use for a short period until 1941, when they were replaced for most journeys by two new vehicles, saloons 798 and 799, to be described in Chapter 3.

Like his father and mother during the 1914–18 conflict, King George VI together with Queen Elizabeth (later Queen Elizabeth the Queen Mother) made considerable use of the Royal Train during World War II and from the surviving

HM Queen Mary. Note the subtle differences of trim, panel details and finishes in what, superficially, appear to be identical compartments. Both these

compartments underwent further changes before the coaches were withdrawn from service.

The London & North Western Railway twin royal saloons of 1902, King's carriage nearer the camera.

records it is clear that the Edwardian saloons were not immediately retired, but were used as occasional standby saloons even after their replacements were in service. They even had new ceramic baths and washbasins fitted in August 1941. At the end of each bath there is painted a horizontal red line, a few inches above the waste outlet. Tradition has it that this was a wartime 5-inch water depth indication as an economy measure, which the King had applied to all royal bathrooms. An equally likely explanation is that they are marks to indicate the safe filling level for a bath in a moving train, water spillage being a clearly understood hazard. A typical instruction at the time read:

'The Carriage and Wagon Superintendent has been asked to provide hot water for Her Majesty's bath to be available about 6.30am on the morning of Friday, September 29th, and the timing of the train is *slowed out* [authors' italics] to enable the bath to be taken in comfort.'

The saloons continued in standby service until well after the war, making their final journeys from Ballater (for Balmoral) to Euston on 28 September 1947 (King's saloon) and 12 October 1947 (Queen's saloon). They had lasted for 45 years and had probably run more miles than all the other royal saloons added together. Like their ancestors, the Edwardian saloons were carefully kept at their home base, Wolverton, for many years after withdrawal and eventually went on public show at the Museum of British Transport at Clapham in 1963 – still wearing their wartime 'austerity' livery. As such they came to York in 1975 and in 1979 were moved back to Wolverton for a complete internal refurbish, repaint and repolish. The King's saloon was also put back into its original splendid external livery and went back on public show late in 1980. Subsequently the heraldic insignia have been re-applied and since then, thanks to a generous grant from the Friends of the National Railway Museum, Queen Alexandra's saloon has been similarly repainted so the coaches may now be viewed in all their original glory.

The East Coast Contribution

So far the story of the preserved royal vehicles has concerned itself solely with those owned by the London & North Western Railway and its lineal descendants who operated the so-called West Coast route to Scotland. However, as has already been mentioned, many other private railways of Great Britain also possessed royal vehicles, varying from individual special saloons attached to normal trains to complete sets of coaches entirely analogous to that of the LNWR. Foremost of the other railways operating complete trains were the Great Western Railway and the East Coast group of companies, the Great Northern, North Eastern and North British Railways. This triumvirate shared ownership of the East Coast Joint Stock (ECJS) carriages used for Anglo-Scottish workings. The GWR contribution was considerable but sadly nothing remains of its early royal saloons, save for a few isolated examples of loose furniture in the National

The tiny, comprehensive kitchen of the Duke of Sutherland's saloon.

57ᴬ SALOON
NOTICE
YOU ARE VERY SPECIALLY REQUESTED
NOT TO THROW ANYTHING OUT
OF THE WINDOW OF THIS
SALOON.

HM Queen Alexandra's LNWR saloon of 1902 is, without doubt, one of the most graciously furnished vehicles ever to run on the railway. The main picture (left) shows the day compartment as now preserved and, essentially, as used by both HM Queen Mary and HM Queen Elizabeth the Queen Mother when they were both Queen Consort.

On the right are two views of King Edward VII's 'other' carriage – East Coast saloon 395 as preserved, showing the day compartment and smoking-room Although taken recently and representing the vehicle as used by Queen Elizabeth the Queen Mother, the superb wood veneers and general décor are the originals from the period 1908–25, when the vehicle was the King's semi-exclusive preserve.

Following page: Various details of the 1902 LNWR saloons as now preserved. The rooms principally featured are the smoking-room (King's saloon) and the bed and bathrooms of the Queen's saloon, the latter as rebuilt in 1941. The remaining view shows the exquisite attention to detail in these vehicles.

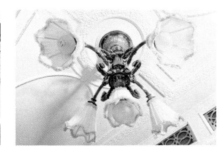

Opposite page:

The East Coast saloons of 1908–9. The top view shows 395 as built, liveried in varnished natural teak; while below is seen 395 as preserved (with the simple external handles and the 1954 'claret' livery). The bottom view shows the preserved 396 (also in 'claret') with the external fittings originally affixed to 395.

Railway Museum Collection. However, the East Coast contribution was also considerable and two splendid saloons have survived.

The East Coast route to Scotland runs from London, via Doncaster, York, Newcastle and Edinburgh to Aberdeen and it may reasonably be assumed that the companies controlling it, later to be amalgamated in 1923 to form the unified London & North Eastern Railway (LNER), were as keen to impress King Edward VII as had been the LNWR. Moreover, one of King Edward VII's favourite residences was Sandringham House in East Anglia, well within the East Coast sphere of influence, so it is hardly surprising that a few years after the emergence of the 1902 LNWR saloons, the East Coast replied in kind with its own sumptuous Royal Train. Like the LNWR ensemble, the East Coast train consisted of a pair of opulent 12-wheel saloons, a set of semi-royals and other supporting vehicles.

The two principal saloons, both preserved, were designed by the famous Nigel Gresley when he was carriage and wagon

superintendent to the Great Northern Railway (GNR). He later became much more celebrated as the designer of a famous series of high-speed steam locomotives and was knighted in 1935. However, his influence in carriage building was equally significant and the preserved royal vehicles pay splendid tribute to this period of his career. Unlike the LNWR built saloons (wholly owned by one company), the Gresley royal saloons were ECJS vehicles. Most ECJS coaches were built in England and because the English part of the East Coast operations was divided approximately in two between the GNR to the south of York and the North Eastern Railway (NER) to the north of that city, Gresley adopted design features from both railway companies in the two royal saloons. Moreover, one each was built at Doncaster (GNR) and York (NER). There was, however, no design influence from north of the Border although the North British Railway did share ownership of the saloons. Doncaster Works was responsible for the subsequent maintenance of both vehicles.

The coaches themselves are massive 12-wheelers. They run on very distinctive chassis fitted with inverted bowstring girder side members. This was essentially the design of underframe used by the NER for its heavier 12-wheel dining cars. The bodies themselves have full height, semi-elliptical roofs and bowed ends. Ceremonial doors are present at both ends of both vehicles and the side panelling is a sort of cross-breed between GNR and NER styling. Essentially the style is NER above the waist and GNR below. The body panels are clad in solid Burma teak and, for some two-thirds of their service life, the vehicles displayed this beautiful wood in natural form but with a highly varnished finish. Natural varnished teak was essentially a GNR trademark but later became the standard for the ECJS and its LNER successor.

In some people's eyes, this marriage of GNR/NER styles is not wholly successful in strictly visual terms. Viewed from certain angles, the carriages can seem to have a slightly top-heavy look which lacks something of the elegance of normal Gresley-designed coaches of more purely GNR/LNER parentage. However, in technical terms they were quite outstanding for their day and the interiors are without peer. Like their LNWR contemporaries, they were fitted out by Messrs Waring and Gillow.

Like the LNWR saloons, the East Coast pair underwent several changes during their long life in service and their prime utilisation changed on more than one occasion. For this reason it is slightly misleading to refer to them simply as the King's and Queen's saloons and it is better to use their running numbers, No 395 (built at Doncaster) and No 396 (built at York).

When new, saloon 395 was for King Edward VII and 396 for his Queen – exactly comparable with the LNWR pair of carriages. However, unlike the LNWR pair, the interior layouts were distinctly different from each other. That of No 395 (built in 1908) was all but identical to King Edward VII's LNWR saloon – a layout obviously to the King's liking – with a similar suite of rooms (dressing-room, bedroom, day saloon and smoking saloon). For wholly day-time journeys, the bedroom could be converted to a dining-room by changing the furniture. The Queen's carriage (396), built a year later in 1909, was rather different from the LNWR equivalent. There was still a large day saloon, adjacent to which was the Queen's bedroom. Beyond these rooms the coach was given a side-corridor arrangement running alongside two lavatories, two small dressing-rooms and a second bedroom for HRH the Princess Victoria. Queen Alexandra's bedroom itself was normally screened off with a moveable partition which, in effect, extended the side corridor arrangement past this room. For day journeys, this partition (and the bedroom furniture) was frequently removed and the area converted to a six-seat dining-room in the same manner as in the King's carriage.

The side-corridor arrangement past the bedrooms was obviously a convenience since it enabled the train staff to

East Coast saloon 395 as built showing
the bedroom and how it could be converted
to a dining-room when required. As preserved
this area is now a (smaller) retiring room.

patrol the vehicle without disturbing the occupants – and this feature was built in to all subsequent royal saloons.

This arrangement of the two vehicles continued in use until 1925 – well into the reign of King George V and Queen Mary – at which time some extensive alterations were made to both of them. It appears very likely (though not entirely confirmed by records available to the Museum) that by this time, virtually all overnight journeys by the Royal Family were made using the 1902 LNWR train – regardless of which railway system was being used – and, in consequence, the East Coast vehicles were increasingly used for day journeys only. The conversions, therefore, took the form of removing the bedroom facilities from both vehicles. It was from this point that the utilisation of the vehicles became confusing.

Saloon 395, the erstwhile King's carriage, now became the exclusive preserve of HM Queen Mary. The main day saloon and smoking saloon remained largely unaltered, save for some minor re-positioning of internal doors, but the former King's bedroom was reduced in length to become the Queen's private saloon. The former dressing-room remained as such but was made longer and given a side corridor alongside for added privacy. There were also slight alterations to the toilet areas. Obscured windows were re-equipped with new glazing carrying Queen Mary's monogram and the exterior handles to the entrance doors were removed and replaced by those from Saloon 396. Originally, No 395 (being the King's saloon) had exhibited more elaborate exterior handles than 396 but the roles were now to be reversed.

The modifications to 396 were equally comprehensive. It now became the principal vehicle of the pair (thus receiving the more elaborate exterior handles) but was designated as 'Their Majesties' Saloon' for the King and Queen travelling together by day. The day saloon remained as such but the former bedroom-cum-dining-room became a private sitting-room.

The suite of dressing-rooms, together with Princess Victoria's bedroom, was extensively modified to produce two larger dressing-rooms with lavatories *en suite* and the King's dressing-room (formerly Princess Victoria's bedroom) was also fitted with a full-length bath.

It is basically in this revised configuration that the two vehicles are now preserved. However, their history was by no means complete with the 1925 conversions; for they lasted in service until the mid-1970s. Furthermore, the interior décor in both vehicles underwent several changes during this period. As originally built, saloons 395/6 were decorated internally in what was described in contemporary records as the Louis XVI style and surviving contemporary photographs clearly indicate that the vehicle décor also had much in common with the LNWR saloons. Most of the interior surfaces were white enamel, save for the day and smoking saloons in No 395 which had wall panelling of polished sycamore (inlaid with pewter and light mohogany) and oak (inlaid with boxwood and dark pollard oak) respectively. These beautiful wood finishes, rivalled in the preserved collection only by the inlaid mahogany panelling of the smoking room in the King's LNWR saloon, have remained unchanged throughout, but the furnishing and interior enamel finishes have undergone several changes in both vehicles.

It is impossible to be dogmatic about these changes, but it does appear that of the various users of the vehicles, HM Queen Mary was the most influential in the choice of colours and replacement fabrics and furniture. Queen Mary is known to have made a particular study of interior decoration and it has already been remarked that she was personally responsible for many changes in décor of the LNWR saloons, although the individual pieces of furniture remained essentially unchanged in these two vehicles.

In view of these known occurrences it seems highly likely that Queen Mary was equally involved with the much more

comprehensive changes in the East Coast vehicles. Not only were several of the rooms substantially altered but carpets were changed, certain items of furniture were replaced and at some time the enamelled wall finishes were changed from white to their present pastel shades with green predominating. There was also at least one, if not two major changes of upholstery pattern on the loose furniture.

One of the reasons for some of the changes was the extraordinary longevity of the East Coast saloons, even after the 1925 re-modelling. They tended to be used less often in the purely daytime role than did the LNWR pair in both a day and overnight capacity, especially during World War II. Consequently there does not seem to have been any degree of pressure to have them replaced during the 1940s unlike the case with the LMS (exLNWR) vehicles. In consequence, 395/6 continued in use in the East Coast Royal Train well into the period of the nationalised railway (1948 onwards). As far as can be determined, in the absence of many of the records (even assuming they still exist), few major changes took place between 1925 and 1952. In the latter year, HM King George VI died, followed in 1953 by the death of HM Queen Mary. These two closely spaced events precipitated further changes in the use and rôle of the Royal Train and this particularly affected 395/6.

The old LNWR saloons were now out of use and HM The Queen and HRH The Duke of Edinburgh took over the use of the still fairly new LMS-built replacements (see Chapter 3). They also continued to use East Coast Saloon 396 as a

Princess Victoria's bedroom (Saloon 396)
as built and as converted in 1925 to a
bathroom-cum-dressing-room. Note the suppression
of much of the ceiling detail after conversion.
The principal day compartment of Saloon
396 as built and as subsequently converted
in 1925. Note the re-positioned door and,
again, the unfortunate removal of the
Adam-style ceiling detail.

joint vehicle for day journeys but, in due course, Saloon 395 became the personal saloon of HM Queen Elizabeth the Queen Mother, as she now was, in succession to Queen Mary.

By now the two East Coast vehicles were nearing 50 years old and almost 30 years had passed since the 1925 alterations. Their teak bodies were still as sound as ever and it seems manifestly clear that the Royal Family thoroughly enjoyed riding in them. Moreover they were the only royal saloons whose dimensions permitted them to run under the sometimes restricted clearances of the Southern Region of British Railways. Additionally, economic circumstances in the mid-1950s were somewhat different from those appertaining in earlier years and it probably made good financial sense to retain them for limited use, rather than build new vehicles. They were, therefore, given further attention, the most striking change being the obliteration of the famous varnished teak finish and its replacement by a dark 'Royal Claret' colour into which, at the Duke of Edinburgh's suggestion, all royal vehicles (from whichever original owning company) were now to be re-painted. This colour, all but identical to the former LNWR carmine lake, was chosen to match the royal motor cars which may themselves, in former days have derived their dark red colour from the old LNWR train – full circle perhaps? The painted finish now given to 395/6 was superb, but many people were sad to see the disappearance of the famous teak graining and it is said there were many long faces in the paintshop at Doncaster when the instructions were first issued.

Other changes were a further re-upholstery of both vehicles, (saloon 395 being refurbished to HM Queen Elizabeth the Queen Mother's directions) and much repainting of the interior enamel panelling. The present satin finish wall colours probably date from this time. Thus, as preserved, the interiors of these two venerable coaches reflect the travelling styles of their final users. They will be kept (internally at least) in this form by the Museum since, as they stand, they carry evidence of all the periods of their long life. In due course, when the present exterior paintwork needs attention, consideration will be given to re-instating the original varnished teak.

The saloons were finally retired, being somewhat incompatible with the 100 mph railway, when the new Royal Train of 1977 was brought into service. They were handed over to the Museum in 1979 and such was their quality that no restoration work at all was necessary to render them fit for public display. Space restrictions at York meant that, initially, only No 395 came to the main Museum but a suitable temporary home for No 396 was offered by the Bressingham Steam Museum near Diss, Norfolk, which was able to meet the Museum's stringent storage and security requirements. It is not inappropriate that one of them should go on public show in East Anglia, not too far from Sandringham, to and from where it regularly operated. However, in due course the Museum hopes to have them re-united in York in company with all the other preserved 'pairs'.

The Supporting Vehicles

From the complexities of the specialised Edwardian saloons in the collection it is almost a relief to turn to the final group of preserved vehicles from the same Edwardian era. These coaches differ from the ones so far considered in that they are 'royal' by association only, having been constructed, originally, as conventional vehicles of the types used in normal trains.

Since far back in the days of Queen Victoria, the operation of royal vehicles has always been a somewhat complex business. Whenever the sovereign travelled by train it was normal to attach to the principal royal saloon(s) a number of additional vehicles to provide for the travelling staff and to service the train itself. None of the supporting vehicles from the Victorian period has survived but, not surprisingly, in view of the comprehensive building of new saloons during King Edward VII's reign, the railways themselves provided a considerable number of additional vehicles, from stock as it were, to operate with these new saloons. Four have survived to be taken into the National Collection, not simply because they possess the 'royal' association but, perhaps more importantly, because they also represent significant stages of development in passenger coaching stock in their own right.

Foremost among them is a superb 12-wheel first-class dining-car dating from 1900. This was built by the LNWR at Wolverton and is contemporary with and in matching style to the Duke of Sutherland's saloon. This style of carriage 'architecture', as one might call it, was highly characteristic of all LNWR dining, sleeping and special saloons and the preserved dining-car is one of more than 130 similar vehicles (including the Edwardian royal saloons) built during the 1895–1905 period. Dining-saloons were built for all classes of passenger so the preserved vehicle may truly be said to be in the mainstream of catering vehicle design at the turn of the century.

Its first association with royal travel cannot be dated with accuracy but the first recorded working traced by the authors was in October 1904 between Ballater and Euston. This may well have been its first royal journey but we cannot be certain. King Edward VII did not share his mother's dislike of eating on the train so it is not surprising that, from this early date, the dining-car was added regularly to the 1902 set of royal and semi-royal saloons. The choice of an existing standard dining-car for royal use may be considered a little unusual, especially in view of the special building of new principal saloons, but the vehicle chosen had good claim to be singled out for more exalted service than its fellows.

Dining-car No 76 (as it is now numbered) was built as one of a series of identical dining-saloons between 1897 and 1901. Most were built for the LNWR but No 76 was actually allocated to the West Coast Joint Stock (WCJS) – a fleet of vehicles jointly owned by the LNW and Caledonian Railways for Anglo-Scottish workings on the so-called West Coast route. At the time it was numbered WCJS No 200. When new it was sent to the 1900 Paris Exhibition, where it won a Grand Prix for its superb finish and fittings. On return it was reallocated to the WCJS. However, unlike all other WCJS dining-cars, it was first-class only and most Anglo-Scottish services provided dining facilities for the lower orders as well. In consequence No 200 was not wholly suitable and was transferred to join its fellow first-class only cars on the purely LNWR system. When the Royal Train needed a dining-car, it was logical to choose one of the newest examples available and, although no written evidence has been located by the Museum, it probably seemed appropriate to let the King

have exclusive use of the Grand Prix winner. Other dining-cars were also used, intermittently, for the next ten years or so to supplement No 200 and by 1917, a second, all but identical car to the King's diner was permanently added to the train for the Royal Household staff and railway officers. This too is preserved, but in private ownership. Its number, latterly, was 77.

Traditionally, most railway dining-cars contain fixed seats, either in facing pairs across a table or facing single seats across a somewhat smaller table. In general, first-class vehicles had fewer seats, usually of more ample proportions. It was common to divide the seating area into smoking and non-smoking areas and the all-essential kitchen and pantry facilities were usually located at one end of the vehicle. The royal dining-car conformed to this arrangement having twenty seats (twelve in the smoking saloon, eight in the smaller non-smoking area). All were arranged as facing singles in conventional first-class manner.

This layout continued in use for some time, but in 1942 the fixed seats were removed from the smaller saloon and a long

Dining-car 76 in the 1954 'royal claret' livery (as withdrawn in 1956) and *immediately prior to re-instatement in the traditional colours in 1978–9. The all-over* *dark finish does not really do justice to the magnificent coachbuilding of this vehicle.*

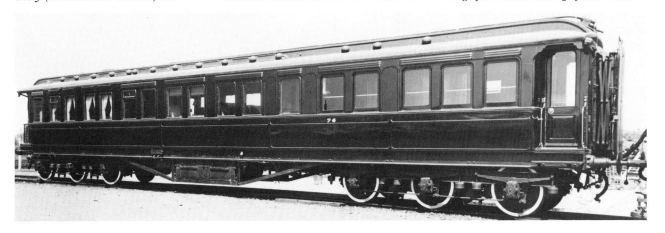

centre table with individual armchairs was substituted to form the main royal dining-saloon. It is surprising that this more logical arrangement (for royal purposes) was not made at an earlier date but diagrams of the carriage and official records of the changes to the vehicle leave little doubt that this was a wartime measure. It is in this form that the vehicle survives.

Within the coach the fittings are sumptuous in the extreme and in no way inferior to those of the royal saloons themselves. The walnut and mahogany woodwork is elaborately and beautifully inlaid with leaf and flower designs. Cornice mouldings have an inlaid repetitive motif, elaborate carved frames and pediments embellish the doorways and the ceilings are of patterned lincrusta. Metal fittings are of elaborately wrought oxidised silver. The original seats (in the 12-seat saloon) are padouk, upholstered in moquette, and the loose chairs are mahogany, upholstered in green patterned silk. What is perhaps most outstanding is that, loose seating excepted, all this decorative embellishment was the norm for *ordinary* passengers at the turn of the century – even the third-class versions of the same type of carriage were hardly less elaborate.

The saloon was renumbered 5200 by the LNWR, renumbered again by the LMS in 1923 as 10400 and received its present number, 76, in 1933. Like the rest of the LMS Royal Train, and by royal request, it retained its LNWR colours (with LMS markings) during the 1920s and 1930s, being repainted, like the royal saloons, in standard LMS crimson lake in 1939/40, for greater camouflage.

By the time King George VI came to the throne, the LMS, in succession to the LNWR, seemed to feel that its Royal Train needed some modernisation. The uncrowned Edward VIII had little affection for the Royal Train but his brother, already a family man, was clearly likely to make far more use of it when he came to the throne after the abdication. The alterations to the principal saloons have already been mentioned (see page 24) but dining-car 76 also came in for treatment. The bodywork was clearly sound but the railway chose to re-mount it on a modern and much more substantial chassis and this was done during 1938/9.

Because of the modernised underframe, No 76 was not replaced in 1941 when the new principal saloons were built. In fact it remained in service until 1956, thus lasting long enough to receive the current 'royal claret' livery just before withdrawal. Like its associated saloons it was kept in store at Wolverton until placed on show in 1963 at the Clapham Museum, finally coming to York in 1975. In 1977 it was taken off exhibition and returned to Wolverton for complete overhaul and repaint, emerging in mid-1979 resplendent in its former LNWR colour scheme and correctly carrying LMS markings as in the 1938–9 period. Later in 1979 it formed the most important element of a Museum train of vehicles, celebrating the centenary of train catering, which performed a 2500 mile tour of Great Britain. Meals were served in the old car again and thousands came to see it. Less than a year later it appeared at the Rainhill celebrations to mark the 150th anniversary of the Liverpool & Manchester Railway (another component of the old LNWR) and was used to convey the VIP party to the opening ceremonies, accompanied by two other support vehicles (see below) and hauled by the Museum's preserved LNWR express steam locomotive *Hardwicke*. One suspects that its travelling days may still not yet be over!

The other three support vehicles in the collection are considerably less glamorous than the royal dining-car but are of considerable historic interest. Two of them are from the former LNWR (later LMS) Royal Train and one from the East Coast equivalent.

Preserved LNWR locomotive 'Hardwicke' hauling the three LNWR Royal Train support vehicles and participating in the 'Rocket 150' celebrations at Rainhill, Liverpool in May 1980.

All are what is known as guard, luggage and brake vehicles – that is they have accommodation for the train guard, they contain luggage space and are fitted with handbrakes to supplement the automatic brakes which were usually applied by the train driver. No locomotive-hauled passenger train may operate without at least one such vehicle in the formation and in the days of the steam railway, two such vehicles were normal, usually positioned at each end of the train.

Dealing with the two LNWR coaches first, these were built in 1905 for normal service. They are all but identical and contain (in addition to the guard's accommodation and luggage space) two first-class compartments and a side corridor for access to the end lavatories. They are entirely typical of ordinary corridor stock of the time but in their original form had relatively few passenger seats by comparison with the luggage space. In this form they appear to have been somewhat restricted in normal use but were ideally fitted for marshalling at each end of the Royal Train, where they were used by the technical train crew and other railway staff (e.g. police and catering staff) who accompany the monarch whenever he or she is travelling.

Often, with the less glamorous aspects of the history of preserved vehicles, exact dates cannot be assigned to individual happenings which are none-the-less known to have taken place. However, in this case it is known that the two LNWR vehicles were converted for Royal Train use by the LMS Railway in 1924–5, although the precise date of transfer cannot be traced. At this conversion, the coaches (which were built with low roofs) were fitted with clerestories to harmonise with the other royal vehicles. They, too, carried the full LNWR colour scheme throughout the 1920s and 1930s. At first the luggage spaces were kept clear of additional equipment but over the years they were gradually modified and altered to meet the changing needs of the train.

As preserved, the vehicles carry their LMS operating numbers 5154 and 5155. They were so versatile that they remained in regular use until 1978–9, thus enjoying the longest service life of any of the preserved royal vehicles. In their latter days they were generally referred to as the Power Car (5154) and the Escort Car (5155), although their strictly accurate nomenclature was and is First-Class Corridor Brake.

Although outwardly identical, the two vehicles functioned in quite different ways. In both of them the passenger compartments were modified to allow them to be set up with fold-away beds for the overnight use of the train crew and both of them retained their guard's brake compartment. Thereafter the resemblance ceased.

In the power brake (5154) most of the former luggage space is now occupied by a pair of diesel generators. These were used to provide electrical power to the Royal Train in order to avoid draining the carriage batteries when standing for any lengthy period. The need for a large supplementary power supply dates from the building of the new air-conditioned saloons in 1941. These could only operate with an auxiliary source of power and a new power car was built to run with them (see Chapter 3). This replaced 5154 on most full Royal Trains whenever the 1941 saloons were used but, in 1942, 5154 was fitted with its own generators to act either as stand-by or to provide power for a second Royal Train formation when more than one train was operated – a not uncommon occurrence. Prior to this date it had merely carried additional batteries in the luggage space to augment those of the train.

The larger picture shows former LNWR first-class brake carriage as LMS No 5155 prominent as the first vehicle of the LMS Royal Train in service on the Great Western Railway in 1938. The smaller picture shows an identical (possibly the same) vehicle at the head of a train of matching coaches in the pre-converted form. Note the lack of clerestory prior to conversion.

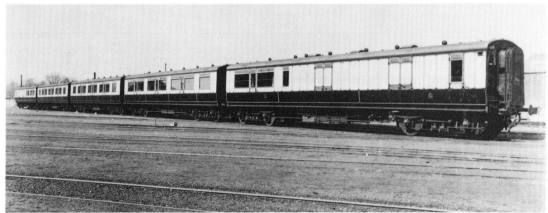

The escort brake (5155) always accompanied the train until replaced by a new vehicle in 1977. In this vehicle, the luggage space was altered at an early date and was equipped with extra water tanks, floor lockers fitted with seat cushions on top, a mess table and a small kitchen. Eventually it also acquired a small office corner and telephone exchange. It was 'home' for the train crew and a sort of 'control room' for the whole operation of the Royal Train.

Like the royal diner, 5154 and 5155 received new chassis in the late 1930s at the start of George VI's reign and continued in use for another forty years – an astonishing commentary on the robust carriage construction of the Edwardian era, for both are basically made of wood.

The two carriages were released to the Museum in 1979, 5154 making the last proper 'royal' journey of either of them in March of that year (with HM Queen Elizabeth the Queen Mother), immediately prior to its repainting (along with 5155) in the old LNWR colours. At the time it was technically in the Museum's possession! Since then the Museum has used them both in their traditional role at either end of its special catering centenary train in 1979 and running with the royal diner 76 at Rainhill in 1980. No 5155, running singly, is frequently used, still as an escort vehicle, in support of the Museum's working steam locomotives. Quite apart from their historic nature, these two vehicles are expected to play a continuing, if occasional, role for some time to come in support of the Museum's outside activities and are not normally to be seen on public show.

The last support vehicle is the East Coast equivalent of 5155 and is, in some ways, more historically important as a Museum vehicle than either of the LNWR brake coaches since it dates from 1908 and is in virtually unmodified condition. Designed, like saloons 395/6, by Nigel Gresley for the East Coast Joint Stock (ECJS) it is, the Museum believes, the oldest surviving Gresley vehicle in substantially

original condition, the pioneer extant example of a highly characteristic and significant coach style.

The East Coast train, like the LNWR version, operated with a brake and guard's coach at each end, the main difference being that the East Coast guard's coaches were full luggage vehicles without any conventional passenger compartments. The surviving example is one of two all but identical vehicles which always operated with the East Coast train, even when new. Nevertheless, they were perfectly conventional and identical to their general service equivalents.

The preserved example was built as ECJS No 82 and later became LNER 109 after 1923. One or two slight modifications during the 1920s have obliged the Museum to restore it with its LNER rather than ECJS running number. However, the basic livery is the same – the celebrated varnished natural teak, lined out in primrose yellow and vermilion. Inside the coach the accommodation is substantially comparable with the facilities already described for 5155. However, because the East Coast train rarely operated in an overnight capacity there was not the need for sleeping compartments for the train crew.

In its latter years (the late 1960s and early 1970s) the vehicle stood under cover and out of use – save as a stores vehicle. Its condition when received by the Museum was, therefore, remarkably good and as restored, its panelling is entirely original, no replacement having been needed. It was transferred to the Museum in 1976 and restored at its original works, Doncaster, in 1977, the paintshop staff being delighted to remove the royal claret colour and replace it with its traditional finish.

The future of No 109 in the Museum is likely to be more static than mobile because of its historic importance, but it would make a suitable location for travelling exhibitions without affecting the original material inside – and this may be its eventual destiny.

Royal Train support vehicles as restored. The main view shows the elaborate door treatment of dining-car 76, while one of the smaller pictures illustrates the dining-car (together with the two first-class brakes) immediately after completion of repainting in 1979. The last view shows East Coast brake (LNER No 109) as restored to immaculate varnished teak at Doncaster in 1977.

*Interiors of royal dining-car 76. The principal view shows the
unmodified 12-seat saloon (with its original seats and tables)
as normally displayed at the Museum in the function of a
'serving' saloon. The upper picture on this page shows the
royal dining-room as converted in 1942 with loose chairs.
Until this date, this end too was furnished in like manner to
the view opposite. The former fixed-seat positions are marked
by plain wood panels on the sides and ends.*

Latter-day simplicity – the King's and Queen's day compartments and the Queen's bedroom of the 1941–built LMS saloons 798, 799.

3 The move to simplicity

The last two vehicles to be considered in this survey stand in marked contrast to the Edwardian carriages which form the bulk of the preserved collection. They are the two principal saloons built in 1941 by the London Midland & Scottish Railway (LMS) and designed under the supervision of William Stanier (later Sir William A. Stanier, FRS).

The vehicles (numbered 798 and 799) were built during the darkest days of World War II and entered service almost surreptitiously – clearly because of the tight security necessary at that time. There is a commonly held belief that they were built because of the wartime conditions in order to give more physical protection to the King and Queen, but recent examination of the official LMS order book indicates that the vehicles were actually ordered as early as 1938. Of course, it may well be that, by 1938, railway management foresaw the likelihood of war and was being prudent; but an equally likely explanation is that by this time, the old LNWR saloons were thirty-five years old, a fair age for any railway vehicle and one which would normally lead the railway company to consider a replacement as a matter of routine. There is considerable evidence that the LMS intended to build a complete new train but, in the event,

only the two principal saloons, along with their power car, emerged.

Mention has been made in the previous chapter of the very long life of the East Coast saloons 395/6 but this was somewhat exceptional and undoubtedly influenced by the much smaller annual mileage covered by the East Coast vehicles. The old LNWR saloons had seen much more service and if their condition prior to their recent 1980 renovation was any guide, the general wear and tear within the saloons was of a somewhat greater order than in 395/6.

Be that as it may, the LMS resolved to build two new principal vehicles and, when they emerged in due course, they were seen to represent a radical departure in visual terms from anything previously associated with the Royal Train. Full details were not released until after the war but by then, their existence was no secret even if their details were.

When built, they were fitted with auxiliary armour plating and steel-shuttered windows – clearly because of the war – and it was, therefore, difficult to appreciate their proper external lines. However, in July 1947, the armour plate was removed and the vehicles were seen to present possibly the smoothest and simplest outline ever seen on a British Railway vehicle until our present day. They were also very heavy – at some 56 tons each, conceivably the heaviest passenger carriages ever to run in Britain. At this weight and fitted as they were with heavy duty 6-wheel bogies, not to mention a considerable amount of sound-deadening material, their riding quality was superb. The authors, having been privileged to ride in them on their delivery to York, can confirm that this characteristic remained until the end of their service life even after reduction in weight to 52 tons each by the removal of the armour plating. The riding sensation is one which seems, illogically, to be almost independent of the rails – they seem almost to float along with a gentle swaying motion, restful rather than unpleasant and almost silently as far as the occupants were concerned.

In this context, it may be remarked that the 12-wheel chassis arrangement combined with a heavy vehicle body almost always produced excellent riding qualities – and we can vouch for the fact that all the preserved royal 12-wheelers have exemplary riding behaviour – but 798/9 are in a class apart at normal 'steam railway' speeds. At the higher speeds beginning to become normal in the mid-1960s, they became rather lively and were, therefore, restricted to 70 mph.

The vehicles themselves are fully in the traditional line of evolution of principal royal saloons although their simplicity of décor can cause the visitor almost to pass them by at first

LMS Saloon 798 (King George VI),
wartime shutters open.

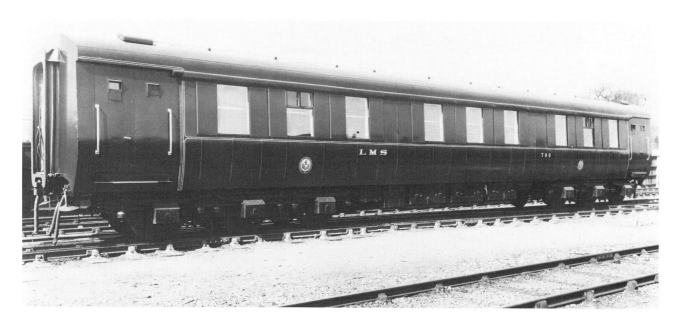

sight – which is a pity, for they are in many respects the most interesting saloons in the whole collection. Like good wine or good music, they need rather longer acquaintanceship to be appreciated to the full.

From the outside the smooth sweep of flush steel panelling is immediately obvious – not for these vehicles the elaborate exterior mouldings and decoration of earlier days. Their visual quality lies entirely in the realm of line and proportion, combined with superlative paintwork. There being so little to distract the eye in the way of external details, any tiny blemish in the finish is immediately obvious and, over the years, great care has been taken to preserve this sleek simplicity. This means coach painting *par exellence* and over the years Wolverton works tended to develop an

almost pathological obsession with the paintwork on these saloons. When they were released to the Museum it was some years since they had been repainted (largely because they were due for replacement) and the craftsmen were concerned that if they were simply displayed as they stood, they would not truly represent a proper 'Wolverton job'. To the casual eye there was hardly a blemish on them but the painters were not satisfied. Fortunately, the Museum had already decided to have them repainted prior to display so honour was satisfied.

The reason for the repainting was quite simple. During their life they carried two main colour schemes, LMS crimson lake from 1941 to 1954 and the current 'royal claret' thereafter. They were so much alike that it was felt both more

LMS Saloon 799 (Queen Elizabeth),
wartime shutters closed.

49

These four views show Royal Saloon 798 under construction at Wolverton in 1940–41. On the left can be seen the massive underframe prior to the adding of the body, together with the first stage of constructing the body itself – the assembly of the timber framing.

On the right the completed timber frame is now attached to the basic chassis (underframe plus wheels) and, finally, the metal skin is added, together with all ancillary 'below floor' equipment, prior to fitting out the interior.

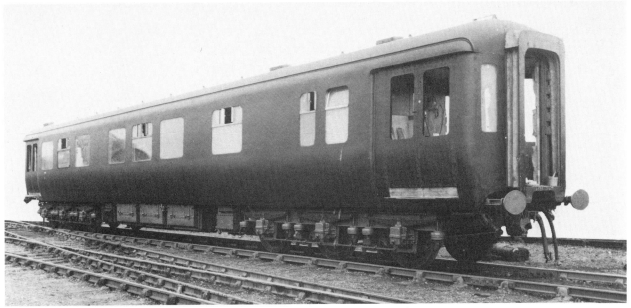

interesting and more historically appropriate to display one vehicle in each of these styles, so a decision was made to repaint 798 in the LMS colour scheme carried when it was HM King George VI's saloon, leaving 799 in the colour scheme used by HM Queen Elizabeth II. The old paint on 799 would, inevitably, contrast with the new finish on 798 so it was resolved to give 799 a repaint as well.

The repainting itself was not without interest and was executed in the traditional coach-painting manner, utilising brush painting throughout and old-fashioned coach enamel paint, not a modern synthetic. This is the method used for all the primary Museum exhibits and the secret of a good finish is to be found almost entirely in the preparation of the surfaces prior to the application of the finishing coats. Something like 80 per cent of the effort and expense is hidden when the task is complete and a measure of the care taken on 798/9 can be illustrated by the fact that the painters applied no fewer than five coats of stopping and filling before they were satisfied that the surfaces were ready for the finishing colour. The object of this preliminary work is to hide all the blemishes. On 798/9 the smooth external surface is achieved by using sheet steel panels but these are fixed to the timber frames by means of countersunk screws and these must then be hidden from sight, as must also the joins between sections of panelling. It all takes time but the end result is the glass-like texture which the vehicles now display.

Turning now to the interiors of these vehicles, their layout is in direct line of evolution from the Edwardian saloons embodying ideas gained, consciously or unconsciously, from both the LNWR saloons and the East Coast vehicles. Unlike their predecessors, however, they are in all essentials identical, the only significant differences being the interior finishes and the fact that the layout of 799 is a mirror image of that in 798.

Both saloons have the traditional double width ceremonial doors at each end; 798 having the window frames in gold finish, 799 in silver. The main entrance lobby leads directly into the day saloon, which is the full width of the vehicle. The King's saloon has upholstered furniture in brown and the Queen's is very similar but in pale grey. From the day saloon a side corridor leads past the night apartments consisting of bedroom and bathroom *en suite*, followed at the far end of the corridor from the day saloon by a small bed-sitting compartment for the valet (King's saloon) or the principal dresser (Queen's saloon). The carriages are completed by the second entrance lobbies wherein are located the electrical control gear and such essential items as an ironing board (King's saloon), a pull-out bed for the footman (Queen's saloon) and a large electric kettle. The inside furnishings for 798 cost £3584 and for 799, £3297.

The coaches are equipped with radio and telephones, the latter being of two kinds. One system was for internal communication between the various vehicles within the train and the other telephone was to connect the train with the national Post Office network when the train was at rest (see Chapter 4). Both vehicles are fully air-conditioned by means of the Stone-carrier system which utilises ice for cooling and steam and electricity for heating. This equipment is rather heavy and is located mostly beneath the floor between the wheels. Servicing the vehicles was a more complex operation than any royal saloons hitherto used. Ice had to be changed at frequent intervals and to maintain an adequate supply of electrical power it was necessary to build a third vehicle of similar size and outline, known as a convertible sleeper, brake and power car. This vehicle (No 31209) contains similar equipment and functions in like manner to that already described (Chapter 2) for power brake 5154, and was retained in service in 1977 as a reserve power car for the new royal saloons.

The style of interior finishing in 798/9 was very much in the fashion of the late 1930s. Soft furnishings, including a very distinctive carpet in the Queen's saloon, came from Marion Dorn Ltd, a famous firm of contemporary designers in New

Bond Street, London, while all the furniture came from Messrs Gordon Russell of Worcester. The ceilings were covered in leather and the decorative wood veneers throughout the two vehicles were chosen from 'selected Empire Timbers', as the LMS was wont to describe them. The LMS made great play in all its carriage interior designs of its use of Empire timber and in 798/9, the usual finishes are Canadian rock elm (799) and lacewood supported by English walnut and weathered sycamore inlaid with white holly (798). The King's saloon embodies much greater use of timber finishes than does 799, which is largely decorated in pastel shades.

Once built, few modifications were made to these two saloons and there was no large-scale re-upholstery or rearrangement of facilities as had happened with the Edwardian vehicles. *The Queen's saloon (799), finally revealed in its sleek simplicity in 1947 after removal of armour plating.*

The only notable change was to enlarge the valet's and dresser's compartments (in 1961) by combining them with the erstwhile separate lavatory compartments to produce a somewhat more spacious bed-sitting area. These enlarged facilities have been retained in both preserved vehicles even though that in the King's saloon was not actually converted until the carriage was used by HRH The Duke of Edinburgh. In the Queen's saloon, of course, it does not signify since this vehicle is displayed in its 1977 livery.

Saloons 798/9 made their first operational journey in June 1941 on the occasion of a visit by the King and Queen to the North-East of England and made their last royal visit in May 1977 to Barrow-in-Furness. They were released to the Museum in 1978 and repainted at Wolverton during that year, finally being placed on public exhibition early in 1979.

4 The Royal Train and its operation

The crew of Queen Victoria's Royal Train prior to its final trip
from Ballater to Windsor on 5 November 1900. The names and
tasks of all the men pictured have survived.

So far, the preserved vehicles have been considered largely as individual elements of a considerable collection, their operation in service having been mentioned only in so far as it is relevant to their story as vehicles. However, the total story would be incomplete without a more detailed look at their rôle in the prime function for which they were built, namely the operation of Royal Trains.

Let it be stated at once that there is no such thing as *the* 'Royal Train'. This fact has caused confusion in the minds of many visitors to the Museum, so it seems relevant to clarify this issue from the outset. The phrase 'Royal Train' is applied, generally, to any set of vehicles which are put at the disposal of the Royal Family and, of course, such a set would usually incorporate one or two of the principal saloons.

However, the exact formation would vary from occasion to occasion and depend very much on the nature of the function attended by the principal traveller. Normally, vehicles allocated for Royal Train use are kept separately from normal service stock and are marshalled as required on each occasion the train is required.

Essentially the requirement of any Royal Train formation is that it should contain sufficient facilities to accommodate not only the member(s) of the Royal Family travelling at the time but also those members of the Royal Household and railway staff whose presence is essential. This basic requirement has remained largely unchanged since the days of Queen Adelaide but the methods by which it has been met have changed down the years.

Put at its simplest, there are, in addition to the royal passengers, three basic groups of travellers to accommodate. Firstly are those members of the household accompanying the principal passenger(s) – and these may well include distinguished VIPs travelling as guests of the Royal Family. The second group of staff is that of the senior railway officers whose function is to act as liaison between the Royal Household and the railway in general. The third group is what is best referred to as the train crew itself. This group will include any or all of such categories as technical staff (responsible for the minute by minute maintenance and servicing of the vehicles), catering staff (when dining vehicles are present) and security staff (railway police), whose task is self evident. In addition to these groups there is finally, of course, the locomotive driver (together with his assistant) and the train guard. These latter staff will not necessarily always be the same people (unlike the other on-train crew members) but are usually selected from more senior employees with a considerable degree of experience and reliability.

Over and above the actual people involved with the train itself are the special working arrangements made by the railway organisation for the safe working of Royal Trains.

The railway is, by its very nature, the safest form of land transportation and accidents are very rare indeed. However, the Royal Train is operated under even more stringent operational rules and has never in all its history been involved in an even mildly serious accident.

It goes without saying that running Royal Trains can be quite an expensive operation and in this context it must be mentioned that this cost is met by the Privy Purse and not by the railway. The vehicles used in the Royal Train actually belong to the railway and the Royal Family, in effect, pays a fare for their use, together with meeting the costs of the additional special arrangements surrounding their operation.

Against this background to operations it is now possible to place the preserved vehicles in context with the operational methods of their day.

Unfortunately, little is known of the ancillary vehicles associated with Queen Adelaide's coach or how her train was operated, but from Victorian times onwards a considerable quantity of recorded information has survived, some of it in the Museum library. These latter records may be studied in detail by prior appointment. Space permits but a brief sampling of them in this book, but even a few examples will, it is hoped, give something of the flavour of Royal Train operations down the years.

In Queen Victoria's time, much use was made of the various royal saloons owned by the different railways but, as already stated, the vehicle which is preserved was her undoubted favourite and seems to have been selected for as many operations as possible. It was always used for the Queen's visits to Balmoral and the journey between Windsor and Ballater (the station for Balmoral) was made at frequent intervals, usually at least twice per year. Its operation was reasonably typical of the time and, although covering the lines of several railways, was basically under the control of the LNWR, the owning company of the train itself.

The operation of the train for Queen Victoria was conditioned by several fixed factors. Firstly, the Queen disliked travelling at more than about 40 mph; schedules, therefore, had to be drawn up to meet this requirement even after the railways were regularly operating trains at higher speeds for ordinary passengers. Secondly, the Queen is said to have disliked eating on the train. As a result, meal stops had to be scheduled. At this range in time it may be doubted whether the Queen had a genuine dislike of eating on the train, for she is known to have enjoyed the use of railway dining-vehicles on her continental journeys by train. One suspects that a more likely explanation of the lack of meal facilities on Queen Victoria's train lies in the fact that British dining-cars, though dating from 1879, had not reached any great degree of refinement until the 1890s. Moreover, to enable passengers to reach the dining-car it was vastly preferable for all vehicles to be fitted with continuous corridor communication and Queen Victoria's LNWR train never was. Thus, even had her train been given a catering vehicle it would have been necessary to stop the train in order to transfer passengers to it from other vehicles. Queen Victoria was an elderly lady by this time and may well have preferred the greater leisure of the traditional meal stops, utilising the more spacious facilities of an elegant refreshment room. At the same time it must also be stated that the scheduled refreshment stops were often quite brief (ten minutes or so) and the possibility that they were sometimes used simply to take food hampers on board the train cannot be excluded.

The aforementioned lack of continuous communication between vehicles was the third fixed element in the operation of the nineteenth-century Royal Train. Once on the move, each vehicle was isolated from its neighbour and had to be somewhat self-contained. Of itself, this lack of continuous corridor was not unusual – few trains had such features until after the turn of the century – but in the context of Royal Train operations the lack of any ability to patrol through the vehicles was clearly a cause of some of the splendidly worded

British Railways Royal Train in steam days in the Lune Valley 1956. By now the 1941 LMS saloons had been supplemented by three new BR vehicles, two of which were in use on this occasion. The contrast between these and the surviving LNWR coaches is most striking.

instructions to Royal Train guards: 'The Guard in the front van must keep his face towards the rear of the Train and be constantly on the look-out to observe any signal that may be given from any of the Guards or other attendants accompanying the Royal Train, and must communicate instantly to the Driver any Signal he may receive.'

How he made such communication without turning his face from the rear is not recorded!

This is but one fixed instruction from a three-page printed foolscap document issued for each separate journey between Ballater and Windsor. The working timetable extended to another three pages and the Queen herself was given a more lavishly printed version of the same timetable carrying decorative gilded borders and the royal coat of arms in colour. To this was regularly added a fully printed side-view engraving (also with coloured decoration) of the precise composition of the vehicles of the train and the people travelling in them (see front endpaper).

This essential pattern of Royal Train operation has continued to the present day although the increasing amenities of the vehicles provided has enabled the train itself to become more and more a self-contained unit – almost a travelling hotel, in fact, with all that the word 'hotel' implies. Thus, increasingly down the years, the reigning monarch has been able to spend

several days on the train, using its facilities as a base from which to mount several consecutive official functions in quick succession without serious loss of amenity. In Queen Victoria's time the Royal Train was basically a very civilised way of enabling the sovereign to move from one place to another – and it still is, of course. But, additionally, it has down the years been used ever more frequently as an integral part of many Royal Visit programmes.

The move to this additional rôle for the train could not be seriously contemplated until continuous communication through the train was available. The first Royal Train to have this facility was that of the Great Western Railway in 1897 – although it did include a much rebuilt version of yet another of Queen Victoria's favoured, but venerable coaches. None of these vehicles survives but, in reality, the first truly self-sufficient set of royal vehicles was undoubtedly that provided by the LNWR for King Edward VII, and its 'travelling headquarters' function was never more vividly demonstrated than during World War I when King George V and Queen Mary made it their home for days on end as they travelled the Kingdom, encouraging and supporting the nation during that critical time.

Unfortunately, although many working notices still exist from the 1904–18 period, the surviving logs of the LNWR Edwardian Royal Train available to the authors do not go back before 1927 so exact details of the first 25 years of its life are not always easily verified. However, photographs and diagrams of the train during the 1902–27 period indicate that during this time its composition expanded somewhat from its original formation. Originally the supplementary vehicles which operated with the principal saloons were confined mainly to a pair of luggage and brake vans (the precursors of the preserved 5154/5) for the train crew and as many semi-royal saloons as required for the rest of the entourage. The insertion of dining-cars has already been covered and the final move was to enlarge the carrying capacity of the train by adding to the fleet several superb first-class sleeping saloons. Not surprisingly, these were usually chosen from the vehicles built in matching external style during the Edwardian period and, eventually, two or three prime examples became permanently attached to the royal fleet.

The effect of the addition of the sleeping cars was to permit more of the compartments in the semi-royal saloons to be used in a day-time configuration, since their occupants could now move at night to the sleeping saloons. This enabled more senior railway officers or Royal Household staff to be accommodated and thus facilitated the use of the complete train on more extensive tours involving a greater number of officials.

An interesting aspect of this extended use of the train during the Edwardian period was the working of a special horse-and-carriage train two or three days ahead of the Royal Train to ensure that the state coaches, their horses, grooms and associated equipment were well settled in before the arrival of the King. In later days, of course, this practice generally gave way to the present custom of meeting the monarch with a fleet of motor cars.

This pattern continued through the 1930s and the old LNWR Royal Train regularly ran in a formation of eleven or twelve heavy coaches. It is the Museum's great pride that it possesses no fewer than five survivors from this train, all in full working order. However, one must deploy a certain degree of imagination to envisage the magnificent spectacle of the full train in its heyday, resplendent behind a highly burnished steam locomotive. Fortunately, some idea of its character can be gained by the fine model of the train built by the late Gavin Wilson of Wormit, Fife, and donated to the Museum by his widow in Silver Jubilee Year, 1977. It has been exhibited on several occasions since then and will form a semi-permanent feature of planned future displays.

The East Coast Royal Train was hardly less impressive in appearance than its West Coast rival, save in terms of the absolute number of vehicles involved; but, as already mentioned, it was far less often involved in the overnight rôle. In consequence it never acquired any additional vehicles beyond the semi-royal saloons and luggage vans with which it was originally equipped. If catering facilities were required it became normal practice with the East Coast train to requisition one of the many fine dining-cars available at the time.

The building of the East Coast train may well have stemmed not only from a wish to emulate the West Coast but also from difficulties caused by operating the new LNWR train on the GNR system. It is quite clear from the records that King Edward VII so liked the new LNWR set that it was used on every possible occasion. One such instance was on 16 December 1905 when the LNWR train was lent to the GNR to work from King's Cross to Worksop. Much of the correspondence for this occasion has survived, including a letter reporting the event afterwards to Mr Park at Wolverton. One interesting sentence reads: '. . . some of the House Guests would travel up with the Royal Train. This necessitated putting on the train some GN vehicles which caused a little bother as some of the guests wanted to get into our train.' The difficulty was probably caused by incompatability of gangway connections and, doubtless, other instances of this kind played some part in the decision to build the new train.

The operational pattern of the East Coast train was, nevertheless, somewhat simpler than that of the West Coast equivalent. It was, of course, the regular choice for journeys to Sandringham from London and was, quite naturally, employed for all day journeys within its own territory. This not infrequently encompassed day-time workings into Scotland (including Ballater) from departure points within the East Coast sphere of influence.

The authors have not been able to locate any detailed logs of the East Coast Royal Train (assuming they still exist) but surviving working notices available in the Museum Library tempt the conclusion that it was much more common for one or two vehicles of this set to be used, attached to normal service trains for rather more informal royal journeys.

Typical of these would be the regular visits by HM Queen Mary to her daughter, HRH The Princess Royal, wife of the Earl of Harewood, in Yorkshire. On these occasions, saloon 395, frequently unaccompanied by any other supporting vehicle, would be attached to a regular King's Cross-Harrogate train with the minimum of pomp and ceremony either at departure or arrival. Saloon 396 would be likewise employed when the King and Queen travelled together on similar less formal occasions – possibly a race meeting at Epsom or some such event.

The onset of World War II led to a new series of morale-boosting tours of the country by King George VI and Queen Elizabeth, just as the King's father and mother had done previously. Once again the old LNWR train was frequently out on its travels for several days at a time but this time there was the additional problem of air raids to concern the operators. It has been seen how this caused the old LNWR train to be painted in standard LMS colours to render it less conspicuous in day time; but a greater perceived danger seemed to be the problem of night raids.

It had long been the custom with the Royal Train, when on tour, to work it as near as possible to its chosen destination the day before an official function, wherever schedules permitted. It would then be 'stabled', usually in some quiet siding, thus enabling the Royal party to enjoy a night's rest on the train without the added disturbance caused by the vehicles being in motion. No matter how fine the carriages, it *is* more restful to sleep in a stationary train than a moving one! During the war, as an added precaution, the overnight 'stabling' points were, as like as not, located close to a convenient tunnel and an engine in steam was kept ready so as to propel the train into the tunnel in the event of an air-raid warning, the tunnel serving in very truth as a 'king'-sized air-raid shelter.

As a matter of interest, the very first working of the two 1941-built saloons (798/9) included just such an operation. The planned visit was to the North-East of England and, on the first day, the train came as far as Crimple Junction, just south of Harrogate, where it was stabled at the north end of Prospect Tunnel on the (now closed) Harrogate to Wetherby

line. The record does not state whether, on that occasion, it was actually run into the tunnel. During the six years of the war, the LMS Royal Train alone was out on 94 occasions (approximately every 3/4 weeks) and saloons 798/9 ran 36,000 miles during this time, so keen was the King to support his nation.

After the war, there were only two principal sets of Royal Train vehicles left in regular use, the LMS (mainly ex-LNWR) coaches and the LNER (East Coast) vehicles, based at Wolverton and Doncaster respectively. The Great Western Railway was rather hoping to build a new train but post-war austerity caused the programme to be delayed after but two saloons (GWR 9006/7) had been built in 1945. These still survive (in 1981) in the stand-by royal fleet and in due course the Museum has hopes that at least one of them may be placed in its care. Latterly they have been used mainly by HM Queen Elizabeth the Queen Mother.

At first, the nationalisation of the railways had little effect on the royal vehicles and it was not until 1954 that the first moves to the present rationalised situation took place. In that year, all the royal vehicles were repainted in a new standard 'royal claret' colour scheme and it was now necessary to be something of a railway historian to be able to identify the vehicles since only their differing shapes provided indication of their company of origin.

By the mid-1950s, some of the old LNWR vehicles were reaching the end of their lives and this, coupled with the fact that HM The Queen had two young children, caused British Railways to institute a modest building of three new vehicles. In a sense, these were the coaches which the LMS had never been able to build (see page 47). One was a replacement dining-car for the now preserved No 76. The other two were in effect, semi-royal saloons to replace some of the old LNWR semi-royals which were withdrawn. One was for the Royal Household and the other for the royal children (Prince Charles and Princess Anne). All three new saloons followed

the visual lines of the 1941 principal saloons and are still in service, having been extensively modernised in 1977 to run with the new 100 mph royal saloons (below). The children's saloon, still frequently used by HRH The Prince of Wales, is still charmingly referred to by the Royal Train crew as the 'Nursery' car, although the facilities provided in it specifically for young children, have long since been removed. They are, however, carefully stored at Wolverton in case of future need.

The next major change was to affect the East Coast train. It made its last journey as a complete set in connection with the wedding of HRH The Duke of Kent at York Minster in 1961, following which, the four semi-royal saloons were withdrawn, along with one of the two luggage vans. The other three (i.e. the now preserved vehicles) were transferred from Doncaster to Bounds Green in London.

The mid-1960s saw the withdrawal of all the residual ex-LNWR semi-royals, ex-LNWR dining-car 77 and the old LNWR sleeping saloons. One of the writers has vivid and somewhat sad memories of seeing these latter vehicles being burned on their frames in 1968. Fortunately, diner 77 and one semi-royal have survived in private hands.

To replace these large-scale withdrawals, a few more modern coaches were transferred to the Royal Train fleet along with a few erstwhile officers' inspection saloons – but in truth the royal fleet was now becoming a bit of a mixed bag. The carriages themselves were still superb but the marvellous consistency of outline of the old LMS and LNER trains had gone. In 1970, the East Coast saloons 395/6 were given their last complete overhaul (for the first and only time at York) and early in 1973 were transferred to Wolverton to join the rest of the collection. The two GWR saloons were similarly transferred so that, for the first time in British railway history there was but one collection of royal vehicles from which to assemble a Royal Train. Nevertheless, a pretty impressive formation could still be mustered and

The LNWR Royal Train waiting at Blackpool for HM King George V and HM Queen Mary on the occasion of the royal tour of Lancashire, July 1913.

HM The Queen alighting from the pre-1977 BR Royal Train and taking the salute at Caernarvon in July 1969 on the occasion of the investiture of HRH The Prince of Wales.

operationally it was far more convenient and sensible to concentrate resources on one location.

The final and current (1981) situation was brought about in Silver Jubilee Year (1977). By now, many main lines were cleared for 100 mph operation but the Royal Train was restricted to 70 mph – its many older vehicles being incapable of operating at higher speeds because their running gear was of an earlier generation. During the early 1970s it became progressively more difficult – and, indeed, inappropriate – to operate the Royal Train in what was fast becoming an obsolete mode. Accordingly, two new principal saloons were built by converting the two pioneer BR Mark III air-conditioned 75 ft long coaches for HM The Queen and HRH The Duke of Edinburgh. New escort and power cars were provided by conversion from modern corridor coaches and many of the older vehicles (including all the BR-built saloons plus a modern dining-car and sleeping car) were uprated for 100 mph operation.

Paradoxically it was this mammoth upgrading of the train plus the building of new vehicles which enabled the Museum to take possession of fully half of its royal saloon collection. Within the space of twelve months during 1978, all three surviving East Coast vehicles, the two LMS 1941 saloons and the two old LNWR support coaches were all transferred to Museum custody, since when, considerable progress has been made in restoring some of them to their former appearance and attempting to complete the gaps in their recorded history.

This book is one of the first fruits of this research attempt but much more remains to be done and, of course, the story is one without any foreseeable end. We are not in a position to say which of the present fleet will ultimately join the preserved collection but it seems safe to assume that the two new principal saloons, at least, will be added to their predecessors in due course. We like to think that when we were privileged to see them under construction in 1976/7, we were, literally, watching history in the making.

Appendix A

Vehicle	Running number	Place and date built	Original owning railway	First used	Last used	Remarks
HM The Dowager Queen Adelaide's Carriage	2	Hoopers of London	London & Birmingham Railway	1842	1849	Chassis built at Wolverton and vehicle may be a little older than quoted – see page 3.
HM Queen Victoria's saloon	LMS 802 (in 1933)	Wolverton 1869	London & North Western Railway	1869	1900	Originally two 6-wheel coaches, rebuilt in 1895 by uniting both bodies onto a new underframe.
The Duke of Sutherland's saloon	57A	Wolverton 1899	Privately owned	1900	1948	Built by the LNWR and generally regarded as the prototype for the 1902 royal saloons.
First-class dining car	LMS 76 (in 1933)	Wolverton 1900	West Coast Joint Stock/ LNWR	Not known (1904 at least)	1956	Transferred to royal fleet from LNWR (ex-WCJS) stock. Extensively modernised 1938/9 including new underframe.
HM King Edward VII's saloon	LMS 800 (in 1933)	Wolverton 1902	London & North Western Railway	1902	1947	Used also by King George V and Queen Mary and King George VI and Queen Elizabeth. Modernised in the 1920s and again 1938/41.
HM Queen Alexandra's saloon	LMS 801 (in 1933)	*ditto*	*ditto*	*ditto*	*ditto*	
HM King Edward VII's saloon	395	Doncaster 1908	East Coast Joint stock	1908	1972	Converted and modernised in 1925 into personal saloon for HM Queen Mary and later used by HM Queen Elizabeth the Queen Mother.

Vehicle	Running number	Place and date built	Original owning railway	First used	Last used	Remarks
HM Queen Alexandra's saloon	396	York 1909	East Coast Joint stock	1909	1977	Converted and modernised in 1925 to dual-purpose saloon for both the King and Queen. Later used by HM Queen Elizabeth II and HRH The Duke of Edinburgh.
Luggage, brake & escort van	LNER 109	Doncaster 1908	East Coast Joint stock	1909	1972	Originally ECJS No 82
First-class corridor brake (power-car)	LMS 5154 (in 1933)	Wolverton 1924–5 – but see remarks	London Midland & Scottish Railway – but see remarks	1925	1979	Transferred to royal use and converted to present form in 1924–5. Vehicles in original form were built by the LNWR in 1904–5 and used in normal service for 20 years before joining the royal fleet.
First-class corridor brake (escort car)	LMS 5155 (in 1933)	ditto	ditto	ditto	1978	
HM King George VI's saloon	798	Wolverton 1941	London Midland & Scottish Railway	1941	1977	From 1952, the personal saloon of HRH The Duke of Edinburgh.
HM Queen Elizabeth's saloon	799	ditto	ditto	ditto	ditto	From 1952, the personal saloon of HM Queen Elizabeth II.

Appendix B

Family Tree of Railways contributing to preserved Royal collection

---

(contributing companies in italic)

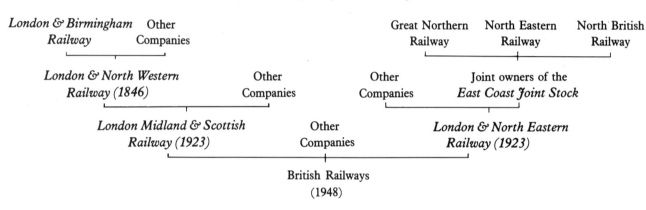

Printed in England for Her Majesty's Stationery Office by Penshurst Press Ltd Tunbridge Wells Kent

     Demand 717055 C120 7/81

Acknowledgements

Much of the information for this book is contained within records held by the National Railway Museum and the Science Museum and we would like to thank our colleagues for their help in searching it out. Most of the photographs, too, are from either the Museum archives or have been taken specially for this publication by the Museum studio photographers, to whom our sincere thanks are also expressed.

We would also like to mention, by name, the considerable help given to us by Messrs N H Campling and J B Dawson of the LNER Study Group in making information available on the East Coast vehicles from their private files. Last but not least we would wish to place on record our considerable indebtedness to the Works Manager of British Rail Engineering Ltd, Wolverton, Mr A G Dungworth, and his staff (especially his office personnel and Royal Train crew) for giving us open access to all surviving records of Royal Train activity at this important establishment.

© *Crown copyright 1981*
First published 1981

HER MAJESTY'S STATIONERY OFFICE
Government Bookshops
49 High Holborn, London WC1V 6HB
13a Castle Street, Edinburgh EH2 3AR
41 The Hayes, Cardiff CF1 1JW
Brazennose Street, Manchester M60 8AS
Southey House, Wine Street, Bristol BS1 2BQ
258 Broad Street Birmingham B1 2HE
80 Chichester Street, Belfast BT1 4JY
Government Publications are also available
through booksellers
A large range of the Museum's publications
is displayed and sold at
The Science Museum, London SW7 2DD
The National Railway Museum
Leeman Road, York YO2 4XJ

ISBN 0 11 290366 5